MADAGASCAR:
THE MALAGASY REPUBLIC

in pictures

Tourism offers a great potential to the economy of Madagascar. This popular resort is on Lake Ampitabe.

By Bernadine Bailey
and others

VISUAL GEOGRAPHY SERIES

STERLING
PUBLISHING CO., INC. NEW YORK

Oak Tree Press Co., Ltd.
London & Sydney

VISUAL GEOGRAPHY SERIES

Afghanistan
Alaska
Argentina
Australia
Austria
Belgium and Luxembourg
Berlin—East and West
Bolivia
Brazil
Bulgaria
Canada
The Caribbean (English-Speaking Islands)
Ceylon (Sri Lanka)
Chile
China
Colombia
Costa Rica
Cuba
Czechoslovakia

Denmark
Ecuador
Egypt
El Salvador
England
Ethiopia
Fiji
Finland
France
French Canada
Ghana
Greece
Greenland
Guatemala
Haiti
Hawaii
Holland
Honduras
Hong Kong
Hungary

Iceland
India
Indonesia
Iran
Iraq
Ireland
Islands of the Mediterranean
Israel
Italy
Jamaica
Japan
Jordan
Kenya
Korea
Kuwait
Lebanon
Liberia
Madagascar (Malagasy Republic)
Malawi

Malaysia and Singapore
Mexico
Morocco
Nepal
New Zealand
Nicaragua
Norway
Pakistan and Bangladesh
Panama and the Canal Zone
Peru
The Philippines
Poland
Portugal
Puerto Rico
Rhodesia
Rumania
Russia
Saudi Arabia
Scotland

Senegal
South Africa
Spain
Surinam
Sweden
Switzerland
Tahiti and the French Islands of the Pacific
Taiwan
Tanzania
Thailand
Tunisia
Turkey
Uruguay
The U.S.A.
Venezuela
Wales
West Germany
Yugoslavia

Throughout the land, the family laundry is done as close to the nearest source of water as possible, in this case, a canal.

PICTURE CREDITS

The publisher wishes to thank Mr. R. Rambahiniarison of the Malagasy Embassy, London, for his assistance in supplying information and pictures used in the preparation of this book. The publisher also thanks the following for pictures used in this book: Bernadine Bailey, London; Minister of Information, Tananarive, Madagascar; Minister of Information, Tourism, and Traditional Arts, Tananarive.

Seamstresses operate their small hand sewing machines out-of-doors.

CONTENTS

1. THE LAND 5
GEOGRAPHICAL SETTING . . . Topography and Climate . . . RIVERS AND LAKES . . . FLORA
AND FAUNA . . . CITIES AND TOWNS . . . Tananarive . . . Antsirabe . . . Fianarantsoa . . .
Tamatave . . . Majunga . . . Tuléar . . . Diégo-Suarez . . . Fort-Dauphin

2. HISTORY 21
EARLY TIMES . . . THE EUROPEANS . . . THE MERINA KINGDOM . . . Radama I . . . Ranavalona
I . . . Radama II . . . Rasoherina . . . Ranavalona II . . . Ranavalona III . . . FRENCH RULE
. . . THE REPUBLIC

3. GOVERNMENT 31
CONSTITUTION OF 1959 . . . POLITICAL PARTIES . . . Strikes and Unrest . . . THE NEW
GOVERNMENT . . . New Constitution . . . EDUCATION . . . WORKING CONDITIONS AND
WELFARE . . . COMMUNICATIONS . . . FOREIGN RELATIONS

4. THE PEOPLE 38
NATIONAL CHARACTER . . . LANGUAGE . . . TRIBES . . . The Merina . . . The Betsimisaraka
. . . The Betsileo . . . The Tsimihety . . . The Sakalava . . . Other Tribes . . . HOMES . . .
FOOD AND CLOTHING . . . SPORTS . . . BELIEFS AND CUSTOMS . . . Mohammedanism and
Christianity . . . Ancestor Worship . . . Famadihana . . . Sorcery . . . THE ARTS . . . Folk
Arts . . . Literature . . . Drama

5. THE ECONOMY 57
AGRICULTURE . . . Rice . . . Cassava . . . Sugar Cane . . . Other Crops . . . Livestock . . .
MINERAL RESOURCES . . . INDUSTRY . . . TRADE AND TRANSPORTATION . . . TOURISM

INDEX 64

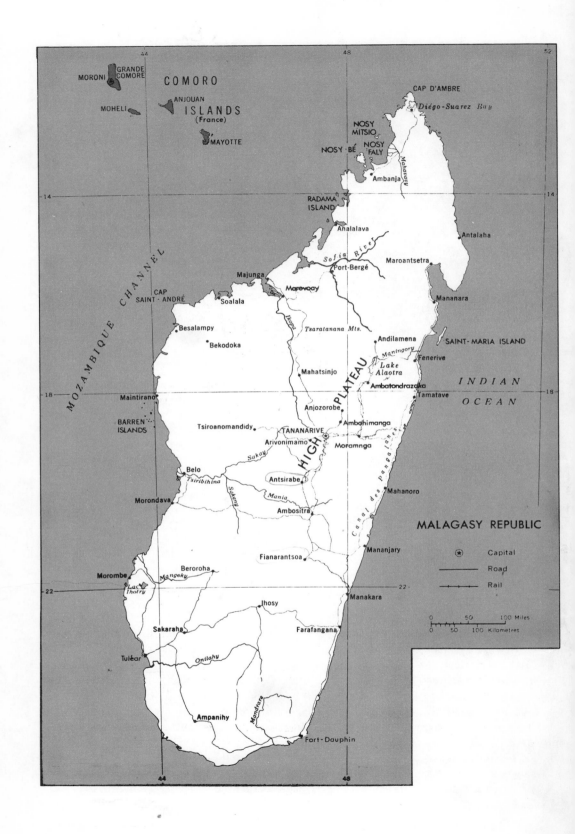

MORONI • GRANDE
         COMORE

ANJOUAN

MOHELI •

COMORO

ISLANDS
(France)

• MAYOTTE

CAP D'AMBRE

Diégo-Suarez Bay

NOSY
MITSIO

NOSY BÉ   NOSY
              FALY

• Ambanja

Mahavavy

RADAMA
ISLAND

Analalava •

• Antalaha

Sofia River

Port-Bergé

Maroantsetra •

Majunga •

Marovoay

MOZAMBIQUE CHANNEL

CAP
SAINT-ANDRÉ

Soalala •

Mananara •

Ikopa

Besalampy •

• Bekodoka

Tsaratanana Mts.

Andilamena •

SAINT-MARIA ISLAND

Maningory

Mahatsinjo •

Lake
Alaotra

Fenerive •

INDIAN

Maintirano •

Anjozorobe •

Ambatondrazaka •

OCEAN

Tamatave •

BARREN
ISLANDS

Tsiroanomandidy •

Ambohimanga •

HIGH PLATEAU

TANANARIVE

Arivonimamo •

Moramnga •

Belo •

Antsirabe •

Tsiribihina

Morondava •

Sakay

Sakeny

Mania

Ambositra •

Mahanoro •

Canal des Pangalanes

MALAGASY REPUBLIC

Fianarantsoa •

Mananjary •

⊛   Capital

_____   Road

Beroroha •

Mangoky

——+——   Rail

Morombe •

Lac
Ihotry

22

Ihosy •

Manakara •

0   50   100 Miles

Sakaraha •

Farafangana •

0   50   100 Kilometres

Tuléar •

Onilahy

Ampanihy •

Mandrare

Fort-Dauphin •

In almost every area in Madagascar outside of the mountains, there are flat, well-watered rice paddies. The word, "paddy," is derived from the Malayan "padi."

I. THE LAND

SHAPED LIKE A GREAT FOOT, the island of Madagascar lies in the Indian Ocean, 250 miles (402 kilometres) off the southeast coast of Africa. Many scientists believe that millions of years ago Madagascar was linked to both Africa and Asia, but there is no conclusive proof of this. Since Madagascar was granted independence from France in 1960, the country has been officially known as the Malagasy Republic.

However, the name, "Madagascar," given by the explorer Marco Polo, is most commonly used for the island itself.

GEOGRAPHICAL SETTING

One thousand miles long from north to south, with an average width of 250 miles (402 kilometres), Madagascar has an area of 228,000 square miles (590,520 square kilometres), making it the fourth largest island in the world. Only Greenland, New Guinea, and

Madagascar has a great variety of climate and topography. The central part of the island, called the High Plateau, has a pleasing combination of hills and lowlands, plus several mountain ranges

Borneo are larger. Slightly smaller than the state of Texas, the island is over two and one half times the size of Great Britain.

TOPOGRAPHY AND CLIMATE

Lying between 12° and 25° south of the Equator, the island is in the tropics, and therefore has two seasons—the hot, or rainy, season from November through March, and the cool, or dry, season from April through October.

The island has three natural geographic divisions made up of a large central highland area and two coastal plains.

The highlands, commonly called the High Plateau (although there are numerous mountain masses), has an average altitude of 3,300 feet (1,000 metres) above sea level. The highest mountain peak, Ambora, in the Tsaratanana Mountains, rises 9,450 feet (2,800 metres) above sea level. The altitude contributes to the pleasant climate in the highlands, which are characterized by warm, sunny days and cool nights throughout most of the year. During the summer months, December to April, there is a total rainfall of more than 50 inches (12 centimetres).

On the east, the High Plateau dips sharply down to a narrow coastal plain, varying from 10 to 50 miles (16 to 80 kilometres) wide. Here it is hot and humid all year round, and more than 110 inches (279 centimetres) of rain fall annually. Great ocean deeps, ranging from 13,000 to 16,500 feet (3,962 to 5,029 metres) lie directly off the east coast. The climate of this coast, where 30 per cent of the population of the island lives, is ideal for the cultivation of such important crops as coffee, bananas, and vanilla. Beset by severe cyclones between January and March, along with frequent floods, the east coast also has a number of coral reefs offshore, creating hazardous shipping conditions.

The fall from the central highlands to the

On the High Plateau, a reforestation plan is underway to replace the trees destroyed by years of extensive stripping of the land and to make room for rice cultivation.

west coast is far more gradual and opens on great rolling plains bordered by the Mozambique Channel, which has an average depth of about 10,000 feet (3,330 metres). The western region has a richer, more productive soil than the eastern plain and supports the cattle-raising industry. However, it is also hotter and drier. The rainfall here is higher in the north than in the south. Rain falls irregularly in the south of the island and often measures as little as 2 inches (5 centimetres) annually in the extreme southwest. The northwest coastline is broken by numerous bays and inlets, while the south coast is almost one continuous line with only a few shallow indentations.

RIVERS AND LAKES

There are many rivers in Madagascar, but only a few make up the 1,550 miles (2,494 kilometres) of navigable waterways. The water-

The wet and humid east coast provides ideal growing conditions for clove trees. Like many other important trees and plants, the clove is not native, but was introduced to the island.

7

Although very few of the rivers in Madagascar are navigable for any great distance, the people can travel a fairly long way by canals and irrigation waterways, propelling their long narrow boats with poles.

shed is less than 100 miles (161 kilometres) from the east coast, and the principal large rivers flow to the west. The rivers flowing down the steep east coast pass through great gorges and ravines where there are numerous waterfalls. On the Sakaleona River there is a 550-foot (168-metre) cascade. The largest river in Madagascar, the Betsiboka, is navi-

The western coastal region is the main cattle-raising area, and is occupied by one of the largest tribes on the island, the Sakalava.

Madagascar abounds in small lakes. Here, the calm surface of such a lake is being disturbed by the wake of a motor launch. The stockade at the right is a large fish-trap.

gable from the west coast for nearly 100 miles (161 kilometres) by light steamer during the rainy season. Other major rivers are the Sofia, the Mangoky, the Tsiribihina, and the Onilahy.

The longest stretch of navigable water in Madagascar is the Canal des Pangalanes. The canal forms a 403-mile (648-kilometre) waterway made up of lagoons that are strung along the east coast and protected by a line of coastal sand dunes. Barges of a capacity up to 50 tons (45 tonnes) can use the canal. However, in recent years, the canal has fallen into disuse except in certain areas. Also, along this coast, there are many ferries that cross the rivers which empty into the ocean.

In addition to the lagoons, there are numerous lakes in Madagascar, but few are large. Lake Alaotra is 25 miles (40 kilometres) long, and the next largest, Lake Kinkony, is 16 miles (26 kilometres) long. The remaining

In the coastal areas, palm trees of various kinds abound, providing welcome shade in the extreme tropical heat.

lakes do not exceed 10 miles (16 kilometres). On the southwest coast is a salt lake, Tsimanampetsotsa, and scattered throughout the island are a number of crater lakes.

FLORA AND FAUNA

At one time, Madagascar was covered with dense forests, but they have rapidly been disappearing. The main reason is that farmers have cut down the trees to make more and more room for pasture land and rice paddies, and there has been no planned system of reforestation. Approximately 15,000 square miles (38,850 square kilometres) of forest land exist at present, and it is estimated that 1,000 varieties of trees can still be found throughout the island.

On the High Plateau, trees, especially pines of various kinds, surround the villages. Most of this area has been stripped of its forest by the practice of *tavy*, which is the burning-off of the land to clear it for rice growing. In certain areas, however, varieties of palms flourish, particularly the raffia palm. The ravenala, called "The Traveller's Tree," which resembles a palm, has received its nickname because a thirsty traveller can break the lower end of a leaf stem and find a small supply of water.

The east-coast tropical rain forests are filled with valuable hardwood trees, along with mangoes, coconuts, and bananas. The most familiar tree on the western plains is the odd bottle-shaped baobob. Many trees are unique to Madagascar; among these are a giant cactus and a triangular-stemmed palm which grows in the Fort-Dauphin area.

It has been claimed that every plant in the world may be found in Madagascar. This is probably an exaggeration, but the fact is that there are many rare herbs used locally in medicine that can be found nowhere else and are practically unknown to modern science. Ferns and orchids abound, along with many other typical tropical plants, a great number of which bear beautiful flowers, such as bougainvillea, jacaranda, hibiscus, mimosa, and nepen these.

The animal life of Madagascar is a delight to tourists, scientists, and, of course, to hunters. Although many of the animals are unique to the island, they are for the most part related to fauna elsewhere, and their individual character is undoubtedly the result of a long period of isolation.

There are no giant mammals such as are found in nearby Africa, and the only rodents are a few varieties of mice. The largest native

One of the most curious looking trees in the world, the baobob can reach enormous proportions. Close to the town of Ampanihy in the southern region of the island stands one specimen whose hollow trunk forms a cavity 9 feet (3 metres) wide and 20 feet (6.5 metres) high.

A profusion of orchids, probably close to 1,000 varieties, is a feature of Madagascar. About 10,000 different plants have been identified on the island.

The crocodile is the largest member of the wild animal kingdom in Madagascar. Plentiful in all of the rivers and lakes, these dangerous creatures, who can move like lightning on both land and in the water, must be avoided by humans.

creature on the island is the crocodile, which is also the only really dangerous one, besides the wild boar.

One of the most interesting animals is the lemur. At least 39 species and sub-species have been identified, most of which are found only in Madagascar. A few relatives exist only in Africa and the Orient. These charming creatures vary from mouse-size to as big as a young child. The grey, short-tailed *babakoto* is the largest. The *aye-aye*, another family member, is nocturnal and only comes out of

Besides the crocodile, the wild boar is the only dangerous animal in Madagascar. This hostile fellow is kept in a deep pit in a zoo. On the whole, the fauna of the island is more related to Asia than to Africa.

These furry babies belong to the large lemur family, for which Madagascar is well known. There are at least 39 species and sub-species on the island.

hiding when night falls. The most common lemur, and one that can be trained, is the *maki*. Although the gentle lemurs are protected by law, considerable poaching exists.

Many kinds of hedgehogs, bats, and civets exist in Madagascar. Various land and sea turtles are also present, as well as lizards, geckos (small nocturnal lizards), chameleons, and snakes. The snakes are all harmless. Crocodiles, whose skins are valuable exports, are found in all waters except in the coldest parts of the highlands.

Madagascar is also noted for its beautiful butterflies, of which there are more than 800 species. In the forest areas, there is an

Another native of Madagascar is this furry white member of the lemur family, the "sifaka," commonly known as Verreaux's monkey.

13

The spoonbill is another wading bird found in the warm, wet forest areas. At one time, Madagascar was the home of a giant flightless bird who mysteriously disappeared about 1,000 years ago. Remains have been found that indicate it stood 10 feet (3 metres) high and laid an egg as big as a football.

One of the first things a visitor might notice in Madagascar is the lack of song birds, especially on the High Plateau where the forest has been destroyed. However, the forests of the coastal regions are alive with birds of other kinds, such as the ibis, who inhabits the swampy areas of the island.

abundance of birdlife—flamingoes, herons, egrets, ibis, owls, and many more.

Such domestic animals as sheep, dogs, pigs, poultry, and zebu (hump-backed cattle) have all been imported to the island in the last few centuries and now play an important part in the life and economy of the people.

For the sportsman, there are wild ducks, wild boars, and crocodiles, and scores of lakes teeming with fish.

Thousands of years ago, huge animals and enormous birds, no longer found anywhere in the world, once roamed the forests and plains of Madagascar. Many giant fossils are still being found and are on display in the museum at the zoo in the capital city of Tananarive.

The most common lemur in Madagascar is the "maki," which can be tamed. Besides carrying its young on its back, the maki is known for swinging from tree to tree throughout the forest.

A number of different kinds of land and sea turtles inhabit the island and its coastal areas, but the only really gigantic species that remain are on the tiny British-owned island of Aldabra, far to the north.

Scientists still do not know when, why, or how these ancient creatures disappeared. Perhaps there was a change in climate and a reduction in rainfall, and the large animals could not withstand the new conditions and thus perished. This is part of the air of mystery that envelops this intriguing island.

CITIES AND TOWNS

TANANARIVE

Tananarive, the capital of Madagascar, is situated in the highlands, half-way between the north and south coasts. The name (*Antananarivo* in Malagasy) means "Town of a Thousand," which dates from the time when the chief, Andrianjaka (1610–30), stationed a garrison of 1,000 men here. Before that it was called Analamanga, meaning "Blue Forest."

This is a city of contrasts: broad avenues and winding lands; high, modern buildings and ancient palaces; up-to-date shops and old-fashioned street markets; modern cars and horse-drawn carriages, alongside zebu-hauled two-wheeled carts. All of these elements add to the charm of this city of 380,000, which climbs and spreads over several hills.

In the middle of the city is lovely Lake Anosy, ringed with jacaranda trees, whose purple blossoms provide an added touch of beauty to the city in the spring. Near Lake Anosy is a newly developed area of the city, boasting modern apartment houses, a large hospital, a 14-storey hotel, a motel with swimming pool and tennis courts, a radio station, and a number of new government buildings. Only a stone's throw away are rice paddies and small farm dwellings, and on top of the hill overlooking it all are the palaces of the former kings and queens of Madagascar and the home of the President of the Malagasy Republic.

Butterflies abound on the island and attract entymologists from all over the world.

15

The old section of the capital, Tananarive, overlooks Lake Anosy. Much of the architecture here reflects the influence of the British on the island. Set on an isle in the middle of the lake is the Soldiers' Monument.

In spite of the many large modern stores in Tananarive, people like to visit the big open-air market, called the Zoma, which is held every Friday on Independence Avenue. Here, almost every necessity is sold—food, clothing, furniture, gemstones, baskets, rugs, and so on.

ANTSIRABE

About 100 miles (161 km.) south of the capital, where it can be reached by either paved road or by rail, is Antsirabe. This town of 60,000 people has become well known as a spa

Some modern "high-rise" housing has made an appearance in growing Tananarive.

Close to Lake Anosy, there is also a newly developed section where there are up-to-date, low-lying, two-family houses.

The weekly market is an important aspect of life in cities and towns. These women of Antsirabe are peddling fruit. Antsirabe, with its numerous spas, is known as the "Vichy" of Madagascar.

Most of the railway stations in Madagascar, such as this one, are modern, and the railways themselves employ diesel engines.

Freighters from many parts of the world are a daily sight in the busy port of Tamatave on the east coast. The beautiful, peaceful beaches surrounding this city belie the hidden dangers of its waters—sharks and strong currents.

because of its hot mineral springs. The name Antsirabe means "Where There Is Much Salt."

FIANARANTSOA

Besides the capital and Antsirabe, the only large inland city is Fianarantsoa, with a population of 48,000. Lying 250 miles (402 kilometres) south of Tananarive in the heart of a large farming area, this city is considered the "capital" of the south. The inhabitants of this area are the Betsileo tribe who are considered experts in the irrigation and cultivation of terraced rice fields. The name, Fianarantsoa, means "The Place of Good Learning." This

city is also connected to the capital by a hard-surfaced road.

TAMATAVE

Along the east coast of Madagascar there are a number of large towns, of which Tamatave is the most important. With a population of 55,000, it is the main port of the island and has road, rail, and air connections to the capital. Tamatave has a large petroleum refinery and is also the point of export for important agricultural products, such as coffee, bananas, cloves, and vanilla. In the Malagasy language, the name of this city is *Toamasina* which

This modern structure in Tamatave houses a Chinese grocery which features a beverage known the world over.

sprang from the name of a Spaniard, San Tomás, who lived there long ago.

MAJUNGA

The major seaport on the northwest coast is Majunga, a city of 50,000, situated at the mouth of the Betsiboka River. However, large quantities of brick-red eroded soil from the highlands are washed into the waters of the bay from the river so that very large ships must anchor offshore. A hard-surfaced road 400 miles (640 kilometres) long runs from Majunga to Tananarive.

People from rural areas are often seen on busy city streets in old horse-drawn carriages.

In small towns and villages, the people live as close to rivers or lakes as possible in order to use their log boats for transportation.

TULÉAR

This city of 35,000 on the southwest coast is inhabited principally by a clan of the Sakalava tribe called the Vezo. These people are fishermen, and the waters of Tuléar are dotted with their tiny out-rigger canoes, while a nearby orange plantation and farms devoted to butter beans provide products for export.

DIÉGO-SUAREZ

Located at the extreme northern tip of Madagascar is this port city of 45,000. Its large, deep-water bay is the largest in the world after that of Rio de Janeiro and makes it an ideal naval base. In addition, Diégo-Suarez has an airport that can take jet aircraft.

FORT-DAUPHIN

At the opposite end of the island, on the southeast coast, lies a smaller port founded by the French in 1642 and named after the heir to the French throne, who was called *Le Dauphin*. This city of 14,000 faces onto many lovely coves and beaches and is surrounded by large sisal plantations.

There are over a dozen other small cities and towns with a population of over 10,000 in Madagascar. The largest of these are Manakara (20,000), Marovoay (19,000), Morondava (18,000), and Antalaha, Ambositra, and Ambatondrazaka, each with 15,000 inhabitants.

Large baskets of grain are a common sight in the village markets in farming areas.

To these shores came the first people known to inhabit Madagascar—the Malayo-Polynesians. No traces of pre-historic man have ever turned up on the island.

2. HISTORY

LITTLE IS DEFINITELY KNOWN about the early history of Madagascar. Arab settlements were made on both the west and east coasts beginning in the 9th century, and the first written records about the island were made by Arab traders. Marco Polo knew of its existence according to his writings on the island of "Madeigascar," but it is doubtful that he ever actually saw it.

EARLY TIMES

The Portuguese explorer Diégo Dias is credited with being the first European to set foot on the island, in 1500. This date also marks the beginning of the Merina (also known as Hova) kingdom. It was the Merina tribe of the High Plateau who were to finally conquer all the other tribes. The origin of the tribes, the

Although long at peace, the Malagasy tribes continue such traditions of the past as carrying these long spears on special occasions.

first known inhabitants of Madagascar, is clouded in mystery, although it is almost certain that they represented mixed Polynesian and African (Bantu) ancestry. It is believed that a Malayo-Polynesian migration to the island probably took place beginning in the 3rd century A.D., ending before the 8th century. How they got there is unknown.

THE EUROPEANS

The Portuguese made efforts to establish a settlement on the southeast coast in 1528, but without success. After a few more attempts, they finally gave up in 1618 and never came back to the island they had named "St. Lorenzo." The British and French also made several attempts to establish settlements along the coast of Madagascar, but were always met with hostility by the tribes, and in the case of the French, were often massacred.

During the late 17th century and early 18th, the Indian Ocean was a popular pirate haunt,

and the base of operations was the east coast of Madagascar. They managed to establish friendly relations with the Malagasy tribes, and some of them settled permanently on the island and became quite influential. One of them even became a tribal chief. Among the buccaneers who made Madagascar infamous at the time was "Captain" William Kidd, who was hanged in 1701.

Eventually, naval activity increased in the Indian Ocean, and piracy gradually died out. However, slave trading flourished during this period in the area and many shipwrecked sailors ended up as white slaves to the Malagasy chiefs. One, Robert Drury, remained in bondage for 16 years.

THE MERINA KINGDOM

Throughout the period of European arrivals and departures, there was great internal strife among the tribes, with one tribe after another taking ascendancy, each subsequently vanquished by another.

In 1787, a member of the Merina tribe was made King at Ambohimanga. He took the name Andrianampoinimerin-andriantsimitoviaminandriampanjaka, which he (fortunately) shortened to Andrianampoinimerina.

The Merina kingdom had been divided into four branches until the end of the 18th century, when the chief, Andrianampoinimerina (1787–1810), united it and proceeded to subdue the other tribes. His aim was to create a unified state in Madagascar and he did much to establish law and order as well as the beginnings of an economic structure.

RADAMA I

Upon the death of Andrianampoinimerina, his son Radama succeeded to the throne, after which there were improved relations with European countries. Radama was a shrewd and enterprising man. Seeing that his people must be educated and civilized, he became friendly with the British governor of Mauritius, Sir Robert Farquhar, who adopted the policy of supporting the Merina kingdom.

Radama made a treaty with Farquhar to abolish the slave trade in return for an annual subsidy of arms, ammunition, and uniforms, as well as British training for his troops. He was thus enabled to establish his authority over a large part of the island. For a number of years, a British agent, James Hastie, lived at Radama's court and helped in advising him.

King Radama I (1810–28) was an enlightened man and strove to perpetuate the goals set by his brilliant father, King Andrianampoinimerina, but he died at an early age. He was buried in a silver coffin made from Spanish dollars.

The missionary craftsmen helped to train the Malagasy people in various trades, and many public works were undertaken. The English government undertook to train 20 young Malagasy in various trades, such as carpentry, blacksmithing, weaving, jewelwork, shoemaking, and so on. Ten were sent to England and 10 to Mauritius.

Although Radama I abolished the death penalty for larceny and certain other offenses, there still existed a law requiring that an officer or soldier who had deserted must be burned alive.

The reign of Radama I was an important period in the history of the country because of the many European influences. Christian teaching was begun in Tananarive by the London Missionary Society. The first school was started by a Frenchman named Robin, and Radama I himself transcribed the Malagasy language into written signs. The English missionaries were instrumental in opening other schools in 1820 and 1821. A printing office was set up and books in English and Malagasy were printed, including fragments of the Bible and a few school books. A Malagasy-English dictionary was printed a little later.

This present-day Malagasy tribesman probably looks very similar to his warring ancestors of long ago.

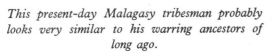

24

Queen Ranavalona I (1828–61) rebelled against European influences that had been encouraged by her predecessors and imposed the death penalty on all who went against her wishes.

The bright prospects thus opening up were clouded by the death of Radama I in 1828, at the age of 36. His death was a great loss to the country, for he had helped to start it on the path of progress.

RANAVALONA I

The crown passed to Radama I's first wife, Ranavalona I, who distrusted the European ideas that were then gaining ground. In 1835, Christian religion was declared illegal. Of the Malagasy Christians, about 200 were killed, while many others were punished by degradation, imprisonment, or slavery.

During Queen Ranavalona's rule there were frequent rebellions, and distant provinces were desolated by wars. Following her husband's policy of expansion, she waged wars against those nearby tribes who had remained independent of the Merina rule, but without any lasting success. Two chiefs in the northwest area asked France for protection, and French troops came in February, 1841.

For some years, all Europeans were excluded and foreign commerce almost ceased. Among the Europeans who remained in Madagascar was a Frenchman, Jean-Baptiste Laborde. He introduced many industries and had great influence with the Queen. The slave trade was resumed and the Queen refused to see the English representative.

When Queen Ranavalona I died on August 16, 1861, there was general rejoicing among the population. Nevertheless, they had to follow the usual customs and keep to the restrictions and painful traditions of a national mourning.

RADAMA II

When Ranavalona's son, Radama II, came to the throne, there was a return of European influence. Catholic missionaries now came to the island, schools and churches were re-opened, and the printing press was started again. Radama II abolished capital punishment, released prisoners, and gave full pardon to all convicts. Christians in prison awaiting trial were released at once. The King signed a concession giving great powers to a French company.

The coronation of Radama II was celebrated in September, 1862, and the King was delighted with the sympathetic assurances given by the head of the French Mission in the name of Napoleon III. Missionaries from both England and France were made welcome, and the people were free to practice any religion they chose.

The well-meaning Radama II had no idea that he was in any danger. He was eager for Europeans to come to his country, convinced that their return would open a new era of prosperity. As proof of his desire, he abolished customs duties, which encouraged dealers in rum to bring large quantities of spirits to Madagascar.

25

(Left) Radama II (1862–1863), a kind and just ruler, was betrayed and strangled to death with a silk cord in his bed-chamber by insurrectionists.
(Right) Radama's widow, Rasoherina, reigned from 1863 to 1868. She was laid to rest in a coffin made from 22,000 silver dollars.

Fearing the overpowering influence of the French company, the men who had helped to bring Radama II to power now turned against him and brought on a palace revolution against the King. He was strangled to death in May, 1863. Because he was popular with the people, however, they were told that he had committed suicide.

RASOHERINA

The crown now passed to Radama II's wife Rabodo, who reigned as Rasoherina, but actual power was in the hands of the Prime Minister and the Chief Commanding Officer, who claimed they had received it from the Queen. The new Queen refused to ratify the agreement with the French company, but she signed treaties with the British, French, and the United States.

More Christian groups now came to Madagascar: Jesuits, Anglicans, Quakers, and Nor-wegian Lutherans. Capital punishment was brought back, and customs duties were also restored. Hospitals and dispensaries were opened under the supervision of Europeans. The influence of the missionaries was greatly increased by the success of a Dr. Davidson, a Scot, in putting down a smallpox epidemic.

The Queen, who had married the Prime Minister, died in April, 1868, and was succeeded by her cousin, Ramona. The Prime Minister, Rainilaiarivony, managed to keep in control of the kingdom for 31 years by marrying the next two queens as well.

RANAVALONA II

Ramona chose to reign as Ranavalona II. One of the new Queen's first acts was to recognize Christianity publicly. She and her husband, the Prime Minister, were baptized in a Christian ceremony. Christianity was gaining greatly in strength everywhere, and in 1869, the

Prime Minister Rainilaiarivony married three Merina Queens in succession, remaining the power behind the throne for over three decades.

government ordered that all idols be destroyed, which was a great blow to paganism. Also during Ranavalona II's reign, there was a deterioration of relations with France.

The Merina now ruled the central part of the High Plateau directly. The kingdoms of the east and northeast were vassals, but the south and part of the west were independent. Although Merina rule would have satisfied British interests in the island, it was not at all satisfactory to the French. Throughout Ranavalona II's reign, British-French rivalry continued. The Queen died of pneumonia in July, 1883, and was succeeded by a young niece.

RANAVALONA III

The last Merina ruler, Ranavalona III, refused to recognize French interests in the northwest part of the island, and war broke out.

This charming house was built for Queen Rasoherina in 1867, only a year before she died. It is now filled with furniture, jewels, and portraits from her reign.

27

to arm and train a domestic army with the help of the British. This caused the French government to send an ultimatum and war followed at the end of 1894.

FRENCH RULE

In 1896, after revolts in various parts of the country, the French Parliament passed a law annexing Madagascar and making it a French colony. At the same time, all slaves in the island were set free, and General Joseph Gallieni was sent from France to take over civil and military command of Madagascar.

General Gallieni abolished royalty, for Madagascar had already been declared a colony of France. Queen Ranavalona III was exiled and died in Algeria in 1917. By 1898, the authority of France had been established throughout the island.

The tribes were all placed under the direct control of French officials, and some Malagasy who were employed by the French administration were given French citizenship. In spite of these measures, there was a growing sense of Malagasy nationality, and after World War II, a nationalist uprising occurred on the east coast.

After long negotiations, a treaty was signed on December 17, 1885, in which it was agreed that the foreign relations of Madagascar should be directed by France, that a French Resident-General should live at the capital, and that Diégo-Suarez Bay and the surrounding territory should be ceded to France.

In 1890, in return for concessions in Zanzibar, the British government consented to recognize a French protectorate over Madagascar. However, the Prime Minister continued

The King's Tomb on the left and the Queen's Tomb on the right contain the bodies of several 19th-century monarchs.

The grounds of the Queen's Palace are entered through this formidable archway. The Queen's Palace, built for Ranavalona I, was first known as the Great Palace of Manjakamiadana.

In spite of the French, a Merina-dominated nationalist movement remained active, and there were many strikes and demonstrations.

In 1946, three Malagasy nationalists were elected to the National Assembly in Paris. On March 29, 1947, revolts broke out in a number of areas of Madagascar. In some regions they were led by sorcerers who urged the destruction of anyone bringing in modern influences. As a result, about 90,000 people were killed, including many doctors and teachers.

THE REPUBLIC

On October 14, 1958, Madagascar's provincial assembly voted to become a self-governing republic of the French Community. The law of annexation was repealed, and on May 1, 1959, Philibert Tsiranana began his first seven-year term as President of the new republic. On January 26, 1960, Madagascar became the fully independent Malagasy Republic.

The last Queen of the Merina kingdom, Ranavalona III, died in exile in 1917. Her remains were finally returned to Madagascar in 1938.

On October 14, 1958, Madagascar was declared the Malagasy Republic. This building houses the Parliament and is just one of several modern government buildings.

The Queen's Palace, an imposing building made of stone, sits atop the highest hill in Tananarive, overlooking the city and its environs.

On a small islet in Lake Anosy stands this monument to the Malagasy soldiers who died in World Wars I and II.

The new complex of government buildings in the capital of Tananarive is in sharp contrast to the rest of the city.

3. GOVERNMENT

THE MALAGASY REPUBLIC is divided into six provinces, which are further sub-divided into prefectures, sub-prefectures, arrondissements, cantons, and communes. Each town is a City Commune with a Municipal Council. The country villages are grouped into more than 700 Rural Communes, with a Communal Council. The voters of each commune elect the councillors, who serve for 6 years. The General Council of each province is made up of the members of Parliament from that province, plus one member from each sub-prefecture elected by the voters. Many French officials have been employed in the central and provincial governments, but they are being replaced by Malagasy as rapidly as possible.

The capital city, Tananarive, is an exception to this system. It has a Municipal Council of 37 members, who elect the mayor of the city.

The traditional council of village elders,

called *fokonolona*, dates back to the time of the earliest kings. Each council still carries out such practical duties as policing the village area and keeping it clean. They also try to control cattle stealing. In a decree published in 1962, they were given official recognition by the government.

CONSTITUTION OF 1959

Although it is being rewritten, the Constitution of the Malagasy Republic, which became law on April 29, 1959, established a presidential régime. The President, elected for 7 years, was declared Head of State and Head of Government, with the right to appoint all ministers. He was also made Commander-in-Chief of the Armed Forces. He had the right to grant pardon for all offenses, although there is no capital or corporal punishment in the Malagasy Republic.

The National Assembly had 107 members elected by universal suffrage. The Senate was composed of 6 Senators from each province (elected by local councils), 12 nominated by government to represent various commercial and workers' organizations, and 6 more named for some special competence.

The judicial system was modelled upon the French system, with certain changes to suit the traditional laws and customs of the Malagasy people. The Constitutional Court examined all laws and watched over elections. The Supreme Court dealt with matters outside the jurisdiction of the lower courts. The Court of Appeal examined all judgments, both civil and criminal. Lower criminal courts dealt with any crimes not subject to a sentence of more than 10 years in prison. Lesser courts sat in each of the six provinces and dealt with civil and commercial disputes.

Philibert Tsiranana became the first President of the Malagasy Republic on May 1, 1959. Re-elected for a third term in May, 1972, he announced his resignation in October of that year.

The Ministry of Health and Social Services, of enormous importance in the new Republic, has its headquarters in this modern building in Tananarive.

POLITICAL PARTIES

From the time it became a republic, Madagascar has had several strong political parties: the Social Democrats (P.S.D.), the National Independents (MONIMA), and the National Malagasy (R.N.M.). A fourth party, made up largely of people of the Merina tribe (A.K.F.M.), held only three seats in the National Assembly, but had been making strenuous efforts to extend its influence throughout the country. It soon became the main opposition party, and controlled the Municipal Council of Tananarive, the capital. In Malagasy politics, differences between tribes and in regional development are as important as party principles.

STRIKES AND UNREST

On March 30, 1965, President Tsiranana was elected for a second term by a huge majority. The Social Democrats (P.S.D.) who ran the government remained firmly allied to the West, while the A.K.F.M. demanded more contacts with the East. At this time the French still held a dominant position in the economy, and through technical assistants and advisers, they were able to exert considerable influence in other spheres besides government.

In 1970, there was political unrest, and in April, 1971, a revolt broke out in the southern part of the country. After it was suppressed, the MONIMA party was declared illegal and its leader was imprisoned. Later in 1971, the Secretary-General of the Social Democrats (P.S.D.), who was the "Number Two" man in the government, was also arrested and put in prison. The A.K.F.M. still held power in Tananarive.

In March, 1972, President Tsiranana was elected for a third term, to start on May 1. On April 24, however, there was a strike of University of Tananarive students which quickly spread to all the secondary schools in the capital. The students demanded educational reforms and the ending of all ties with France. The movement gained wide support and soon became national.

The government closed the University and sent 400 students to a detention island. The

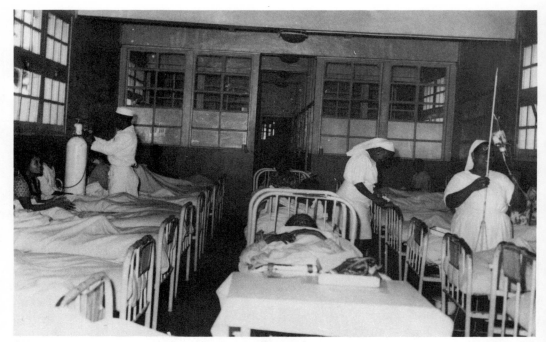

A brand-new hospital has been built alongside the government buildings in Tananarive. The rate of population growth has increased greatly in recent years due to the control of various diseases. Here, nurses minister to children in a crowded, but modern, hospital ward.

resulting upheaval and conflict caused more than 30 deaths and many injuries. The town hall was burned and the government was forced to bring back the exiled students. There were demonstrations and a general strike in the capital which quickly spread to other towns.

On May 18, 1972, President Tsiranana was overthrown, and General Gabriel Ramanantsoa was given authority to form a new government.

THE NEW GOVERNMENT

General Ramanantsoa, as Head of Government, announced that he would form a nonpolitical government and he would introduce a régime of austerity and reform. Accordingly, he reduced the number of ministers in the government from 40 to 10; he released all political prisoners; he abolished certain taxes; and he broke off all talks with South Africa at government level. He also granted more power to the *fokonolona*, the traditional council of village elders.

A national committee was formed, composed of teachers, students, workers, and unemployed. Seminars were held all over the country to prepare for a National Congress. The Congress was held in Tananarive in September, 1972, and voted many fundamental reforms. It was agreed that a new constitution would be drawn up and that new general elections would be held within five years. Meantime, there would be no National Assembly and no President during those five years. On October 8, 1972, a referendum was held and the people voted overwhelmingly for this plan.

On October 11, President Tsiranana announced his resignation as President of the Malagasy Republic.

NEW CONSTITUTION

Details of the new Constitution, as promised by the referendum of 1972, are not yet available. It will no doubt include many of the resolutions adopted by the National Congress of that year. These proposals include the

Since the French left the island, Malagasy has been the language of instruction in the elementary schools. However, the French language persists on the higher levels.

election, by universal suffrage, of a President and a one-chamber Parliament. The President, however, is to be only the Head of State, while the government itself will be headed by a Prime Minister.

EDUCATION

Only half of the young people in Madagascar go to school, and most of them do not go beyond the elementary grades. About 11 per cent of those attending school go on to some form of secondary education. The modern University of Tananarive was opened in 1961 and offers a wide range of courses. About 4,000 students attend the Colleges of Law, Letters, Science, and Medicine that make up the University. There are also eight lycées and institutes of scientific research and agriculture. Classes are conducted in the Malagasy language and in French.

Throughout the country, about 50 per cent

This school in Antsirabe is typical of the new schools being constructed in various parts of the island.

35

In a rural area, children trudge off to school along a dirt path. The Malagasy people set great store by education and make every effort to see that their youngsters receive as much as possible.

of the men can read and write, but only 30 per cent of the women. It is not easy for the government to provide enough schools, because of the rapid increase in population. It is expected that the new government will break away from the French system of education and will introduce a new procedure that is better adapted to the particular needs and goals of the Malagasy nation. This will have to be done in such a way as to give equal opportunity to all, with special provision for children in poorer families.

Eventually, Malagasy will be the language of instruction in all schools, and French will be taught simply as a foreign language. Malagasy is already the language used at the primary level of instruction.

WORKING CONDITIONS AND WELFARE

The official working week is 40 hours, but people in government offices work 44 hours, and farm workers put in a 48-hour week.

Holidays are given on the basis of one-and-one-half days for every full month of employment.

Employers pay a sum equivalent to 13 per cent of each person's salary to a national fund that provides for family allowances, pensions, and industrial accidents. Another 3 per cent is paid to provide for medical services. In general, hospital medical services are free, but there are also wards for which payment must be made. No unemployment pay is provided, and the assistance given to the old and poor is very limited.

There are various charity organizations, both public and private, including the Red Cross and societies for lepers, the blind, victims of tuberculosis and polio, and for mentally handicapped children. Also several orphanages exist, some of them run by the churches.

Medical services include 10 hospitals and 300 medical aid groups and infirmaries. The organized fight against disease has succeeded in wiping out all cases of plague and in reducing the prevalence of malaria.

At the NASA station near Tananarive, these antennae transmit commands to the satellites.

COMMUNICATIONS

The government controls both radio and television and also numerous publications, including an organ of official government information. Many newspapers are published, but some are only a single sheet with a very small circulation. The largest paper is the *Madagascar Matin*, written in French, but containing a few columns in Malagasy.

FOREIGN RELATIONS

The Malagasy Republic is represented in France by an *haut réprésentant*, and in certain other countries by ambassadors. Since independence, the Republic has strengthened its relations with the United States. It has also become an associate member of the European Common Market, the United Nations, and the Organization of African Unity.

After it became a republic, Madagascar undertook reforms to restore its world markets in coffee, sugar, and vanilla, receiving aid from France as well as from the World Bank. The Republic demonstrated its independence in 1967, however, when it ignored French advice and allowed British planes to use the island's facilities to bolster the blockade of Rhodesia.

When the new government was formed, diplomatic relations were established with Russia, China, North Korea, North Vietnam, and Guinea, but relations with Formosa were broken off. Negotiations were begun for a new accord with France, which was signed in Paris on June 4, 1973, the 13th anniversary of Malagasy independence, and came into force on June 26th.

Coffee is of great importance on the island since it is the chief item of export. This man is packing coffee beans in preparation for marketing.

Bead necklaces and raffia articles are on sale in this community market. The life of the majority of the people in Madagascar is not based on the individual, but the group. The group is of extreme importance, whether it be the family, the village, or the "fokonolona."

4. THE PEOPLE

MANY PEOPLE think of Madagascar as part of Africa, but the Malagasy people are not Africans. Some of them like to say, "We are not Africans. We are not Asians. We are something different." And so they are, representing a mixture of Polynesian, Indonesian, African, Arabian, Chinese, and Indian.

The population of Madagascar is close to 8,000,000. Of this number, approximately 100,000 are non-Malagasy, with 31,000 people of French nationality. In recent years, the population has been increasing at the rate of 2 per cent a year, a high figure brought about by the controlling of malaria and other diseases. This is reflected in the fact that about 3,000,000 people are under the age of 14.

NATIONAL CHARACTER

Although the island has had a number of waves of immigration from foreign lands as well as internal movement among the tribal groups, there are certain attitudes and characteristics that prevail among all the peoples.

The family is of extreme importance in Malagasy life. However, the word "family" does not only include the immediate members, such as it does in most European societies. The family in Madagascar includes not only grandparents, uncles, aunts, nephews, nieces, but as many cousins as it is possible to count. Close cousins are treated as though they were brothers and sisters. Family meetings are often

This young Malagasy in tribal finery shows decidedly African Negroid characteristics. There is some speculation that the original Malayo-Polynesian immigrants came by way of East Africa, but there is no certainty of this.

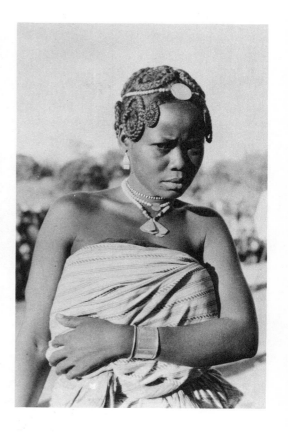

held, and the oldest members are always heard first and carry the most weight. Young people simply sit quietly and listen out of respect.

Although the man is always the acknowledged head of the Malagasy family, women are actually influential, but not on the surface of things. The birth of a boy is of much greater importance than that of a girl. However, because girls are expected to look after their younger brothers and sisters, they generally develop stronger initiative and decisiveness at an earlier age than boys, traits that last throughout their lives.

Friends also are extremely valuable to a Malagasy, and even the most insignificant occasion calls for a visit. There is an island expression that points this up—"It is better to lose money than friendship."

The Malagasy do not have the same concept of time as do most Americans and Europeans. The latter think of time as a straight line going

A former "Miss Malagasy" exhibits her skill at weaving and also her pronounced Eastern ancestry.

The long thick hair of many Malagasy girls is frequently arranged in heavy plaits.

back into the past and forward into the future, and therefore, must keep close track of time in order to get things done before they reach a certain point along that line. A Malagasy thinks of time as a circle with himself in the middle. In other words, he is surrounded by time, and what cannot be done today can always be done the next day.

Most Malagasy people do not even own a watch or clock. Life in the country is geared to the seasons, and the sun is the common time-piece. People get up when the sun rises and go to bed when it sets. After dark, not a light can be seen shining anywhere in the small towns or villages. However, on the warm east coast, the people do not close up their houses as tightly at night as do those living on the High Plateau, and it is possible to see a few people moving about after dark.

On the whole, the Malagasy are rather suspicious of strangers, but they are always polite, hospitable, and friendly. Most villages provide a hut where a passing stranger can spend the night. If one is not available, the village chief will order a family to move out and make their home available, complete with a clean mat on the floor, to the stranger for the night.

The Malagasy is extremely polite. A stranger passing by this man refreshing himself by the roadside, would undoubtedly be greeted, perhaps by "Manao ahoana, tompoko?" This means "How are you, sir (or madam)."

This little pig is on the way to market. The head of the household in Madagascar is officially the man. However, Malagasy women hold a position of much greater importance in society than in similar cultures. This couple, both bearing burdens, are off to peddle their goods.

LANGUAGE

The two official languages in Madagascar are Malagasy and French. Although there are many tribal groupings, the people all speak one common language—Malagasy—in spite of the fact that there are many dialects. French is at present the language of instruction in the schools and is used in both government and business, so that almost every Malagasy can understand it.

Malagasy is of Malayo-Polynesian origin, but over the centuries, the various tongues brought from other lands, along with isolation from its roots, have made it a language in its own right. Its 21-letter alphabet is written in roman script and its characteristic long words of many syllables are rich in metaphors and poetic images. For example, the simple English

A proud mother and her son display a mixture of racial characteristics.

Malagasy women are as expert as men in the cultivation of various crops. Here, two women are giving their offspring an early introduction to the care of cassava plants.

word, "dusk," in Malagasy is *maizim-bava vilany*, which literally translated means, "dark the mouth of the cooking pot."

Family names have meanings, too, and some names reveal British influence, often with the prefix *Ra* added, as in Rajohnson. *Ra* at the beginning of a great number of names is a prefix of respect, much like the English "Esq." or "Mr." For example, a young boy might be called Ikoto, but when he is grown up, he will be Rakoto.

TRIBES

Although the Malagasy form one nation with one language and culture, there are 18 different tribes which are officially recognized by the Government. The tribal groupings represent the old island kingdoms, rather than an exact ethnic division. In addition, there are several clans such as the Vezo and Zafimaniry, which have fairly large numbers, but are part of the membership of major tribes. Despite the fact that the tribes differ in certain ways, the Malagasy say, "All who live under the sun are plaited together like one big mat."

THE MERINA

The largest tribe, with an approximate population of 2,000,000, the Merina were the ruling class before the French took control of the island. They live on the High Plateau and their name means "People of the Highlands."

Mostly of Malayo-Polynesian ancestry, they vary from ivory-skinned to very dark. The women characteristically have very long black hair. At one time, the Merina were divided into three castes: nobles, freemen, and slaves. Long abolished by law, the caste system nevertheless still influences Merina society.

The Merina tribe were the first people to show skills in architecture and the working of mineral deposits. They also invented the very important long-handled spade which is the principal farm implement.

THE BETSIMISARAKA

Numbering well over 1,000,000, "The Many Inseparables" live mainly on the east coast, in the Tamatave area. The second largest tribal group, these people believe in ghosts, mermaids, and little wild men of the woods called *kalanoro*. For the most part, they are engaged in rice cultivation or are employed on the vanilla plantations in the region.

THE BETSILEO

The third largest tribe, the Betsileo, or "The Many Invincibles," populate the southern part of the High Plateau near Fianarantsoa. There is also a large group in the Betsiboka region of the northwest coast. These people are experts in irrigation and cultivation of rice fields and use an ingenious method of preparing the soil—

they simply chase their zebus round and round until the hooves break up and soften the earth. Women are considered the experts at handling the planting and care of seedlings. The Betsileo are greatly influenced by sorcerers, some (*mpamosavy*) who exhibit bad traits and others (*ombiasy*) good traits.

THE TSIMIHETY

"Those Who Do Not Cut Their Hair" derived their name from a time long ago when, in order to exercise their independence, they refused to cut their hair to show mourning for a Sakalava king. These energetic people are grouped principally in the north central area. The most famous tribal member is Philibert Tsiranana, the first President of the Malagasy Republic.

They are the fourth largest tribe with a population of about 560,000.

THE SAKALAVA

Dark-skinned and possessing decidedly Polynesian features, these curly-haired tribesmen number 435,000. Living in the west between Tuléar and Majunga, their name means "People of the Long Valleys." Once the largest and most powerful tribe, they are now cattlemen, and a wealthy tribesman might own as many as 1,000 head of zebu. The Sakalava women hold a much more important position in society than in any other tribe on the island.

OTHER TRIBES

All of the tribes in Madagascar are interesting in that each has its own rituals and beliefs, as well as life style. For example, one group, the Mikea, were a subject of controversy for centuries and are still mysterious. For some time, their very existence was questioned. However, there is definite evidence that they live in small bands in the southwest, near Lakes Namonty and Ihotry, although they have no contact with the outside world. It is believed that they subsist on roots and dwell in small bark shelters.

Another tribe, the St. Marians, occupy the island of St. Maria. Although of Indonesian origin, they represent a considerable mixing

DISTRIBUTION OF TRIBES

Although there is some movement of the tribes, this is the general distribution of the various tribal groups in Madagascar.

with the Arabs, along with other nationalities introduced during the pirate era. This island, ceded to France in 1750, was the only French settlement that lasted. The St. Marians have a dual nationality—Malagasy and French.

The remainder of the tribes are the Antaifasy, Antaimoro, Antaisaka, Antankarana, Antambahoaka, Antandroy, Antanosy, Bara, Bezanozano, Mahafaly, Makoa, Sihanaka, and Tanala.

HOMES

The kind of houses people live in on the island varies from region to region. However, they are all oriented according to Malagasy religious beliefs. Nearly always rectangular, the

43

These women who show the varied characteristics of the Malagasy tribes, nonetheless share a common practice of painting their faces. Tribal customs are tremendously varied on the island.

In northern Madagascar, houses are often built of straight poles arranged like a palisade.

Among certain tribes, elaborate hair styles are the custom on important occasions.

The Vezo, a clan of the Sakalava tribe, characteristically dwell in these wigwams, which are very similar to those of the early American Indian. Fishermen, they inhabit an area on the west coast from Marondova to Faux Cap in the south.

typical house runs from north to south, with the door on the west. Each direction has a special significance for the Malagasy people. For example, the north represents power, the south bad influences, and the east is sacred.

Girls with jugs balanced on their heads emerge from a typical stone dwelling of the High Plateau region.

Two-storey clay houses are a feature of the Tananarive area.

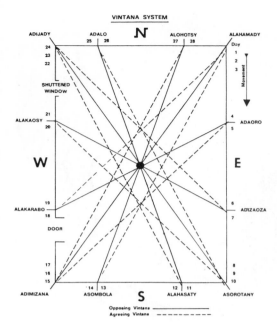

VINTANA SYSTEM

The traditional way of building a Malagasy house is in relation to the points of the compass. The months each have their allocated spot as do the 28 days of the lunar month. This is known as the Vintana System, and the entire arrangement of every article in the house is based upon it.

FOOD AND CLOTHING

The Malagasy diet varies from place to place, according to what is produced locally. Rice, of course, is the most important food everywhere in the island. Cassava, sweet potatoes, coconuts, beans, and tropical fruits and berries add some variety, along with a green vegetable called *bredes*, which is similar to spinach, and fish.

Despite the presence of beef, poultry and pork, these are consumed only on special occasions. In addition, milk and eggs are rarely a part of the typical diet. The lack of these foods has led to general protein and vitamin deficiencies.

The national drink is called *rano vola*. This is made by adding water to rice that sticks to the bottom of the cooking pot and boiling it. Hot or cold, it is thirst-quenching, and is a good drink for the traveller in the countryside since the water has been boiled.

A trip from one end of the country to the other would reveal the great variety of clothing worn by the Malagasy people. In fact, everything from a loincloth to a European suit and dress can be seen.

The Malagasy always sleeps with his head towards the east, never the south.

On the High Plateau, most of the ordinary houses are made of brick or mud. Some are large and have two storeys, while others are one-room huts. In the coastal areas, houses are made of wood, bamboo or fibres. Most of the houses on the east coast are built on stilts or piles.

Furnishings are simple, and the rush mat is used in place of a bed. Often there are no tables, chairs, or other articles of furniture.

This Malagasy family is enjoying dinner on the customary rush mat which serves for sitting and sleeping as well.

The homes of the better-off families will have a few pieces of furniture and perhaps a separate kitchen. However, the cooking area or hearth will always be on the south side of the house so that the flames of the wood fire will combat evil influences.

Cooking is done over an open fire in the majority of Malagasy homes. There are "fady," or taboos, governing the choice of food on every day of the week. For example, it is "fady" to eat anything white on Wednesday.

A lady shops at the local butcher market. Meat and poultry, however, are only rarely consumed by the average Malagasy.

Wealthy Malagasy have such luxurious houses as this. However, no matter how educated and exposed to worldly ideas a Malagasy may be, traditional customs and beliefs are likely to hold sway.

The "lamba," worn somewhat like a Mexican serape, is the national garment. Custom decrees that a woman must have long hair to wear one.

This Malagasy lady wears a combination of Eastern and Western garb, plus the traditional "lamba."

Men often wear a long garment called *malabary*. The most common garment, worn by both men and women, is the *lamba*, a long piece of cloth that is draped over the shoulders and across the chest. Along the west coast, women often wear sarongs. Many people go barefoot, but nearly everyone wears a hat or other head covering. Straw hats, made by hand, vary from the wide-brimmed one worn by the Merina to the cone-shaped, rolled-brim hat of the Bara.

SPORTS

Most modern-day sports are popular in Madagascar—soccer, rugby, volleyball, basketball—and the country has produced a few outstanding athletes. However, the national pastime is a more sedentary one—a game called *fanorona*, which is played on a board divided

The National Women's Basketball Team trekked to Africa in 1960 and captured the Championship.

A game of "fanorona" often will attract as large a crowd in Madagascar as any team sport.

into 32 squares and having a number of diagonal lines. Each player has 22 pieces, most often pebbles. It is a game of skill similar to checkers (draughts).

BELIEFS AND CUSTOMS

Religion in Madagascar is an extremely complex and varied affair. Along with traditional Western and Eastern religious beliefs is a mass of different kinds of ancestral customs and taboos (called *fady*), plus sorcery, all of which

Volleyball, as well as most sports—football, rugby, and so on—are commonly played on the island.

These powerful wrestlers are performing before a rapt audience.

This Catholic church in Tananarive overlooks Lake Anosy. The greatest number of Christians on the island are Catholics, numbering about 1,400,000. They are almost exclusively concentrated in the central High Plateau.

This mosque is in Tamatave. The number of Moslems is estimated at about 80,000. The first outside religion brought to Madagascar was Islamic.

affect every aspect of the daily life of the Malagasy people.

The root of the Malagasy idea of religion is animism, and the most important single influence is that of ancestor worship.

MOHAMMEDANISM AND CHRISTIANITY

The first outside religious influence to affect Madagascar was brought by Arab traders in the 9th century. Today, it is estimated that about 80,000 Moslems live in Madagascar.

Christianity was introduced to the island about 1818 by the London Missionary Society from England, later followed by Catholic Jesuit missionaries, and Anglicans, Lutherans, and Quakers. These various religious groups had a marked effect on the historic and social development of the country. They all established schools as well as churches, and today about 3,000,000 people in Madagascar are Christians, nearly half of them Catholics. Nonetheless, it must be remembered that for a Malagasy, it is perfectly possible to attend church and at the same time subscribe to traditional pagan ideas and customs.

ANCESTOR WORSHIP

Long before Christianity was introduced to the country, the Malagasy believed in one Supreme God, "Andriamanitra." Even though this belief is still held, it is to the *razana*, or ancestors, that tribute must be paid. It is the razana who control everything, from a poor rice crop to a happy event. Death does not mean that a person has left the family. In fact, in death one has enormous power and influence, and those left behind must do everything they can to avoid being disrespectful to the departed ones.

Ancestor worship, regardless of the distasteful nature of some of the customs surrounding it, does give a certain stability to this rapidly changing society. The family tomb is the focal point of the family, and probably the worst thing that could happen to a Malagasy is not to be buried with the family.

The cult of ancestor worship is accompanied by sacrifices to the dead. Some sacrifices are made at special times of the year, such as the beginning of a good harvest, others at a wedding, burial, building of a new home, and

51

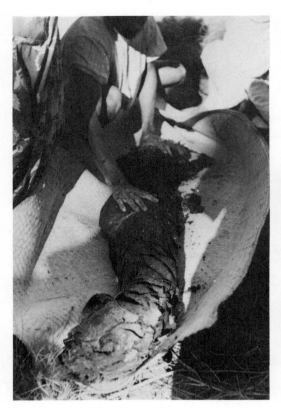

The exhumation ceremony is carried out periodically by families who can afford it. After a body is removed, it is washed and cleaned, and assured by various family members how much it is missed and ←   revered in death.

The remains, along with the old shroud, are wrapped in a fresh shroud made from raw silk.

so on. Sacrifices can be made to ask for something or to offer thanks for something. The offering can vary from a pot of honey to an ox.

Ancestor worship involves the observance of a vast number of taboos, or *fady*. The man at the head of a household is the pivot round which everything must turn. No one may eat before he does, and a young man is not supposed to wear shoes if his father is still alive. It is taboo for a son to build his house north or east

The ancestor, replete in his new finery and having been tossed up in the air, is taken for a stroll round the village before being returned to his tomb.

The tombs of the Mahafaly tribe, who number 120,000 and who inhabit the southwest desert area, are most unusual. "Aloalo," carved wooden posts, are set on the tombs. Often the horns of sacrificed cattle are then placed atop the tombs.

of his father's, and he must not build one that is larger than his father's.

Taboos can relate to plants, animals, tombs, birds, water, or almost anything else. For example, a cock which crows after sunset must be killed; a house must not be built next to a waterfall or a lake which gleams in the sun; nothing green must be burned in the summertime; and on and on.

FAMADIHANA

Famadihana, or the exhumation ceremony of the dead, is a Merina custom. Tombs are dug into the ground, but may also rise as high as 10 feet above it. Made of stone or cement, they contain three tiers of stone shelves on three sides. Bodies, wrapped in shrouds, are placed on the shelves according to their position in the family.

The government has decreed that an exhumation can take place only during the cold season, and a tax must be paid for every corpse exhumed.

The entire family, plus a great number of friends, are invited to attend the ceremony, which can often last several days. The body is carried out of the tomb and into the village on a new rush mat. If the shroud round the body has rotted, the bones are washed and wrapped up in a new raw-silk shroud.

After being taken for a ride round the village or nearby rice fields, sometimes to the musical accompaniment of such a lively tune as "Roll Out the Barrel," the remains are returned to the tomb. The entire occasion is one of gaiety, dancing, and feasting, and can be exceedingly expensive. Families have been known to sell cattle or mortgage their farms in order to carry out such a ceremony.

SORCERY

Various forms of sorcery are important in Malagasy life, particularly in country areas. Local sorcerers, or "witch-doctors," exercise their knowledge of plants and herbs not only for healing, but also for causing some harm.

Sacrifices, particularly of zebus, have been carried out on the island since earliest times, and there are many occasions which call for them.

Basically, there are two kinds of witch-doctor—good and bad. The good ones can supply charms against all kinds of misfortune as well as prescribe plants for healing purposes. The bad ones, called witches, prepare poisons and have an evil influence. They are active when someone in a village is very ill, or if there is a death. They are always attracted to a house where there is a corpse.

In addition, there are fortune-tellers, called *mpisikidy*, who can provide healing charms, and astrologers (*mpanandra*) who advise people on when it is the best time to do certain things.

THE ARTS

The cultural life in Madagascar is dominated by folk arts, literature, and the theatre.

FOLK ARTS

The Malagasy set great value upon their folk music and dances, and a special government commission has been set up to do nothing but foster their development.

If you visit any village, even the smallest along the east coast, you will hear the sound of music and dancing in the evenings, probably

Traditional dances are passed on from generation to generation as this young dancer illustrates.

The "Mpilalao" are
companies of folk dancers
and singers.

from an accordion playing the most popular tune of the day, such as "Vivavy Roozy."

The *mpilalao* are troupes who wear picturesque costumes and specialize in traditional songs and dances, mostly inspired by biblical themes and folk tales. The *mpilalao* troupe is generally made up of two percussion instruments, two or three violins, a clarinet, six lady and six gentlemen singers and dancers dressed in 1850 costumes, and the leader of the troupe. The leader is usually the son or descendant of another *mpilalao*. Scarcely a traditional festival or public occasion can go by without their making an appearance, and meantime they play in the theatres in the capital.

Of all the traditional instruments, the *valiha* is the most beautiful and best accompaniment for the human voice. It has a long bamboo

Women sing at a ceremony
to the accompaniment of
a Malagasy drum.

*One of the most important
days in the year in the
Malagasy Republic is
"La Fête de la République,"
which is the celebration of
the birth of the Republic.
Dancing, singing, feasting,
and many other festivities
take place throughout
the country.*

trunk with several fine metallic cords stretched across it which, when plucked, produce the sound.

Although wood-carving is the prime artwork of the people, there are a number of native painters, such as Ramanankamonjy, Ranivoson, and Coco Rabesahala. Two important artist societies in Tananarive organize exhibitions and gallery showings.

LITERATURE

As the bookshops and libraries in the capital attest to, Malagasy has its own literature. Since Malagasy was first transcribed by the king in 1820, poems, essays, and stories have never ceased to appear in print.

The greatest poet in Malagasy history is considered to be Jean-Joseph Rabearivelo, who died in 1937. Other well known authors include Jacques Rabemananjara and Flavien Ranaivo.

DRAMA

The Malagasy theatre is of recent origin and first began with enactments of biblical subjects such as "The Nativity." Malagasy plays are always accompanied by singing. There are a number of theatrical groups, including the Analamanga Theatre, the Antananorivo Theatre, and the Telonoharefy.

*The Malagasy people love music. This man is
playing a Malagasy-made violin.*

Rice cultivation is the major agricultural occupation. To prepare the land for planting, the soil is turned over with a spade, for it is much too wet for successful plowing.

5. THE ECONOMY

AGRICULTURE

The Madagascar economy is essentially an agricultural one, and 85 per cent of the people live in rural areas. However, although 8 per cent of the island's surface can be cultivated, only about 3 per cent is under cultivation at present. Farming methods are most often primitive, with the long-handled Malagasy spade the principal implement. Although the land is often divided into small family plots, in some areas share-cropping is practiced.

RICE

The most important crop is rice which is grown mostly for home consumption, although a special variety of high quality has been developed for export. (Actually, the rice cultivated in South Carolina in the late 17th century was begun with rice imported from Madagascar.)

The rice-growing area in Madagascar has been doubled in the last few years. Rice is cultivated on the island in three ways: in normally irrigated fields; in marshy areas that do not require irrigation; and on dry land where the forest and bush have been burned off.

In the irrigated fields, the yield is about one ton per acre, although on some of the large fields in the Lake Alaotra area, up to four tons per acre have been harvested in a single season. However, compared to Japan's yield, which is often 10 tons per acre, this is not high. On the cleared lands which, after one crop has been grown, require a number of years to return to fertility, the yield rarely rises above half a ton per acre.

The entire rice-growing cycle—preparing

Everyone helps in the arduous job of setting out the rice plants in the water-covered land. Sometimes a frame is used to make sure the plants are set in a straight row.

Sugar cane is grown on large plantations as well as in small areas by individuals. Here, a Malagasy farmer is taking his small harvest to market.

the field, planting, cultivating, and harvesting— takes from 120 to 150 days every year.

CASSAVA

The second largest crop is cassava, which becomes the staple food in the Malagasy diet during years of poor rice harvests. About 82,500 tons (74,894 tonnes) are produced each year. Most of the cassava is consumed locally, but a certain amount is processed and exported in the forms of starch and tapioca.

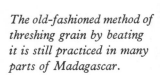

The old-fashioned method of threshing grain by beating it is still practiced in many parts of Madagascar.

Tobacco-growing is under the strict supervision of the government. These men are cutting the tobacco to size and bundling it, preparatory to shipping.

SUGAR CANE

Introduced into Madagascar about 1800, sugar cane can be grown in any area that has an altitude of less than 4,000 feet (1,300 metres). Most of the sugar plantations, however, are along the northwest coast, especially on the island of Nosy-Bé. Much of their crop is exported, sugar being the fourth most important export product.

Small farmers also grow their own sugar cane on little plots and frequently use it to make a fermented drink, *betsabetsa*. Close to 100,000 tons (90,780 tonnes) of sugar cane are harvested each year.

OTHER CROPS

Coffee is the chief product of the east coast of the island and is the most important export as well, accounting for more than half of the revenue brought in from foreign trade. In 1973, the coffee quota on the world market accorded to Madagascar was 83,000 tons (75,347 tonnes). In an average year, well over 50,000 tons (45,390 tonnes) are shipped out to foreign ports. In spite of the importance of coffee, there are only a very few large plantations, and the main source of coffee is the small planter.

Second in importance as an export crop is vanilla, introduced into Madagascar in the middle of the 19th century. Vanilla cultivation has expanded so greatly along the east coast that the Malagasy Republic is now the world's leading producer. Cloves, ground nuts, and lima beans are other important agricultural products much in demand by foreign markets. Along the east coast many tropical fruits are raised, but bananas are the only fruit exported. Sweet potatoes and potatoes are grown for local consumption in areas over 4,000 feet (1,300 metres). Other important products are perfume plants, peanuts and manioc yams.

Among the non-edible crops are tobacco, which is under a government monopoly, and sisal and cotton. Most of the 40,000 acres (16,188 hectares) of sisal cultivation is in the southeast of the island, near Fort-Dauphin. Much emphasis is now being placed on cotton, which was brought to Madagascar in 1900, and might prove to be a valuable product if its cultivation is expanded. Most of the existing cotton fields are along the southwest coast.

LIVESTOCK

Several hundred years ago, African hump-backed cattle were brought to the island. Called zebu, they now make up most of the estimated cattle population of 10,000,000. The zebus are used mainly as beasts of burden with their principal duties being those of tilling and hauling. An average zebu yields only half a gallon (2 litres) of milk a day; however, the Malagasys drink very little milk, perhaps a little over a gallon (4 litres) a year per person. There is a strain of cow known as *rana* in the Tananarive area which has a higher yield.

In spite of the fact that the more zebus a man has the richer and thus more important he is, a

Although there are machines used in Madagascar to harvest grain, they are generally owned by large companies.

certain number are sacrificed according to the prevailing cult of ancestor worship.

For the most part, in the main cattle-raising regions, the herds wander about at will. At slaughter time, many of them have to be driven as far as 300 miles (480 km.) to Tananarive, which can take as long as several months and result in a great weight loss. The potential boost that the cattle industry could offer to Madagascar's economy has yet to be explored.

Pigs, first brought to the island by early Portuguese explorers, are found everywhere. Sheep are raised mostly in the extreme southwest. In the south and west, Angora goats provide milk, as well as the raw material for mohair rugs. Geese, ducks and chickens are kept by most villagers, supplying eggs and main courses at important family celebrations.

MINERAL RESOURCES

Madagascar has been called a "land of samples" because so many different kinds of minerals exist on the island, but only in small quantities. Gold occurs in minor alluvial deposits in the north near Diégo-Suarez, but minor amounts only have been recovered. Gold panning is practiced by some of the people in the area.

Raffia is an important crop, but to be useable it must be torn by hand into narrow strips as this man is doing.

Although it is estimated that there are low-grade coal reserves of over 700 million tons (635,460,000 tonnes) in the Sakoa River area, exploitation has not yet begun.

Madagascar is one of the world's largest producers of graphite. First discovered in the highlands, new veins have now been found south of Tananarive on the east coast. This mineral is used chiefly in the electronics industry, but unfortunately the demand for it has lessened in recent years. Chromite is another very important mineral, and as much as 105,000 tons (95,319 tonnes) are exported in a year, particularly to the United States. Mica deposits are found chiefly in the south, and more than half of the annual production is sold to the United States.

Other important mineral resources include phosphate, uranium, and thorium, plus valu-

Because of the many semi-precious stones found in Madagascar, gem-cutting and polishing has become a thriving industry.

able nickel deposits which are being investigated near Moramanga.

Madagascar is probably best known, however, for its semi-precious stones, found in great variety and quantity. The most popular stones are amethysts, beryl, garnets, moonstones, and tourmalines.

Although an oil refinery was opened at Tamatave in 1965, no oil has been discovered on the island despite extensive exploration efforts. The refinery keeps busy, however, with crude oil brought from other countries for use in Madagascar.

INDUSTRY

Most Malagasy industry and manufacture is closely tied in with agricultural products, for example, sugar refining, tobacco curing, meat preserving and tanning. Most cotton weaving takes place near the cotton fields. The largest industry is the refining of sugar which takes place on the northwest coast on Nosy-Bé and at Majunga, where the cane is grown on land developed by irrigation. Abundant water-power exists throughout the island, and two large river dams supply electricity in the area of Tananarive.

There are also factories for processing ground nuts to produce edible, or cooking, oil, and in the south, where sisal is grown, textile works have been opened. Silk weaving and furniture-making are minor industries. Small crafts such as ceramics, lace-making, basketry, and so on, are being encouraged by a special crafts society formed for just that purpose. Other light industries produce goods such as matches, shoes, hats, plastics, soap, cement, elastics, and liquor, as well as sweets, cakes, and soft drinks—all for the local market.

Bricks are made by hand from native clays and are left out-of-doors to dry in the sun.

61

The rail line from the capital of Tananarive to the east coast offers spectacular views and breathtaking descents through deep valleys and long tunnels.

TRADE AND TRANSPORTATION

All in all, the Malagasy economy is expanding, with the GNP (gross national product) increasing at the rate of 6 per cent annually, and with imports gradually going down, and exports going up each year. Distance from foreign markets, lack of funds for investment, a shortage of skilled technicians, and fluctuating world market prices for agricultural products are all problems that must be solved by the Republic.

Most of the trade at present, both imports and exports, is with France and other members of the European Economic Community (EEC). Crocodile skins for ladies' handbags and shoes are a unique export, going mostly to France. Trade with Great Britain is very limited, but the United States buys about 24 per cent of Madagascar's exports. All products for export must be shipped a long distance, and this is a handicap because of the high cost of freight. The comparative lack of domestic industry means that most manufactured goods must b[e] imported.

The basic currency unit of Madagascar [is] the Malagasy franc (FMG).

In the early days, all transport was by foo[t] and goods were slung at two ends of a po[le] which was carried across the shoulders. No[w] there is a road network covering a tot[al] distance of 22,000 miles (35,398 kilometres[)] but as yet only 2,500 miles (4,023 kilometre[s] are tarred and only 350 miles (563 kilometre[s] are covered with stones. Most of the roads a[re] not surfaced at all. As a result, many sma[ll] towns are practically isolated during the rain[y] season.

Today, people travel mostly by *taxi-be*, [a] large car holding seven or eight passengers, [or] by *taxi-brousse*, a local bus seating about 2[0] with standing room for as many as can b[e] jammed in. Some of these buses travel lon[g] distances and will carry anything from peop[le] to hens, goats, or baskets of fish. They ofte[n] have little slogans painted on the side, such a[s]

"God is protecting us." Considering the condition of the roads and the buses themselves, this is highly appropriate.

Madagascar has 532 miles (856 km.) of narrow-gauge railway. The main section, opened in 1909, runs from Tananarive to Tamatave, while branches go north to the Lake Alaotra region and south to Antsirabe. There is also a section from Fianarantsoa to Manakara on the east coast.

Air transportation is extremely important, and Air Madagascar serves many communities. Five airports on the island are large enough to take jet aircraft, and scheduled flights go direct from Tananarive to Europe, Africa, and to the nearby islands of Réunion, Mauritius, and the Seychelles.

TOURISM

Now that flight facilities are good between Madagascar and Europe and Africa, the government is making a special effort to attract tourists. The capital, Tananarive, has a number of hotels and restaurants, plus various attractions that are out of the ordinary. Best of all, it has a practically perfect climate.

In other parts of the island, lake and ocean resorts provide the kind of restful atmosphere—without noise, congestion, or pollution—that many travellers are seeking. For the sportsman, there is fine fishing and hunting, as well as sailing and swimming, and for shoppers many bargains, such as gemstones of great beauty at low prices. All in all, visitors are likely to be highly pleased with Madagascar and come away with the feeling that the Malagasy people are right in calling their homeland "The Happy Isle."

The southwest coast offers a long line of broad, sandy beaches and a dry, sunny climate.

The lush east coast of Madagascar suggests Polynesia—even to the sarongs of these young women.

INDEX

AGRICULTURE, 57–60
Airports, 63
Aldabra, 15
Aloalo, 53
Ambatondrazaka, 20
Ambohimanga, 23
Ambora, 6
Ambositra, 20
Analamanga, 15
Ancestor worship, 51–53, 60
"Andriamanitra," 51
Andrianampoinimerina, 23
Andrianjaka, 15
Antalaha, 20
Antananarivo, 15
Antsirabe, 16–18, 35
Arabs, 21, 43, 51
Area, 5
ARTS, 54–56
Aye-aye, 12–13
Babakoto, 12
Bananas, 6
Baobob, 10, 11
BELIEFS AND CUSTOMS, 50–54
Betsabetsa, 59
Betsiboka River, 8–9, 19
Betsileo tribe, 18, 42–43
Betsimisaraka tribe, 42
Birds, 14
Boar, 12
Bredes, 46
British, 22, 23–28
Butterflies, 13, 15
Canal des Pangalanes, 9
Capital punishment, 24, 25, 26
Cassava, 58
Caste system, 42
Cattle-raising, 7, 8, 59–60
Christianity, 24, 26–27, 51
CITIES, 15–20
Climate, 6–7
CLOTHING, 46–49
Clove trees, 7
Coal deposits, 60
Coffee, 6, 37, 59
Communes, 31
COMMUNICATIONS, 36
Congress of 1972, 34
CONSTITUTION OF 1959, 32
Constitution of 1972, 34–35
Cooking, 46, 47
Courts, 32
Crocodile, 12, 13
Currency, 62
CUSTOMS, 50–54
Dancing, 54–56
Death, idea of, 51
Dias, Diégo, 21
Diégo-Suarez, 20, 60
Drama, 56
EARLY TIMES, 21–22
ECONOMY, 57–63
EDUCATION, 35–36
EUROPEANS, 22
Exhumation ceremony, 52–53

Exports, 57, 59, 60, 62
Facial painting, 44
Factories, 61
Fady, 47, 50, 52–53
Famadihana, 53
"Family" group, 38–39
Fanorona, 49–50
Farquhar, Robert, 23
FAUNA, 10–15
Fianarantsoa, 18
Fête de la République, 56
FLORA, 10–11
Fokonolona, 32, 34, 38
Folk arts, 54–56
FOOD AND CLOTHING, 46–49
FOREIGN RELATIONS, 37
Forests, 7
Fort-Dauphin, 20, 59
French, 22, 25–28, 33, 37
French language, 35–36, 41–42
FRENCH RULE, 28–29
Friendship, 39
Gallieni, General George, 28
Gems, 61
GEOGRAPHICAL SETTING, 5–7
GOVERNMENT, 31–37
Graphite, 60
Great Palace of Manjakamiadana, 29
Groups, 38
Hair styles, 40, 44, 48
Hastie, James, 23
Health care, 34, 36
High Plateau, 6, 7, 10, 40
HISTORY, 21–29
HOMES, 16, 17, 43–46, 47, 48
Hova kingdom, 21
Ibis, 14
Independence, 29
INDUSTRY, 61
Judicial system, 32
Kalanoro, 42
Kidd, William, 22
King's Tomb, 28
Laborde, Jean-Baptiste, 25
LAKES, 9–10
  Alaotra, 9, 57
  Ampitabe, 1
  Anosy, 15, 16, 30
  Kinkony, 9
  Tsimanampetsotsa, 10
Lamba, 48, 49
·LAND, 5–20
LANGUAGE, 35–36, 41–42
Lemur, 12–13, 14
Literacy rate, 35–36
Literature, 56
Livestock, 59–60
London Missionary Society, 24, 51
Mahafaly tribe, 53
Majunga, 19, 61
Maki, 13, 14
Malabary, 49

Malagasy language, 35–36, 41–42, 56
Malayo-Polynesians, 21, 22
Manakara, 20
Mangoky River, 9
Markets, 16, 17, 48
Marovoay, 20
MERINA KINGDOM, 21, 22–28
Merina tribe, 21, 33, 42, 53
Mikea, 43
MINERAL RESOURCES, 60–61
Missionaries, 24, 25, 26
Mohammedanism, 51
Morondava, 20
Mozambique Channel, 6
Mpamosavy, 43
Mpanandra, 54
Mpilalao, 55
Mpisikidy, 54
Music, 54–56
Names, 42
National Assembly, 32
NATIONAL CHARACTER, 38–40
National Independent party, 33
National Malagasy party, 33
NEW GOVERNMENT, 34–35
Nosy-Bé, 59, 61
Oil refinery, 61
Ombiasy, 43
Onilahy River, 9
Orchids, 11
Padi, 57
Palm trees, 9
Parliament building, 30
PEOPLE, 38–56
Pirates, 22
"Place of Good Learning," 18
Plants, 10
POLITICAL PARTIES, 33–34
Population, 38
Ports, 18–19, 20
Portuguese, 21, 22
President, 32
Queen's Palace, 29, 30
Queen's Tomb, 28
Rabearivelo, Jean-Joseph, 56
Rabodo, 26
Radama I, 23–25
Radama II, 25–26
Railways, 17, 62, 63
Rainfall, 6–7
Rainilaiarivony, 26–27
Ramanantsoa, General Gabriel, 34
Ramona, 26
Rana, 59
Ranavalona I, 25, 29
Ranavalona II, 26–27
Ranavalona III, 27–28, 29
Rano vola, 46
Rasoherina, 26, 27
Ravinala, 10

Razana, 51
REPUBLIC, 29
Rice, 5, 57–58
RIVERS, 7–10
Roads, 18, 19, 62
"St. Lorenzo," 22
St. Maria island, 43
St. Marian tribe, 43
Sakalava tribe, 8, 20, 43, 45
Sakaleona River, 8
Senate, 32
Sifaka, 13
Silver House, 28
Slave trade, 22, 23, 25, 28
Social Democrat party, 33
Sofia River, 9
Soldiers' Monument, 16, 30
Sorcery, 53–54
Spoonbill, 14
SPORTS, 49–50
Strikes, 33–34
Sugar, 58, 59, 61
Taboos, 47, 50, 52–53
Tamatave, 18–19, 61
Tananarive, 14, 15–16, 30, 31, 60, 61, 6[?]
Tavy, 10
Taxi-be, 62
Taxi-brousse, 62
Theatre, 56
Time, concept of, 39–40
Toamasina, 18–19
Tobacco, 59
Tombs, 51, 53
Topography, 6–7
TOURISM, 63
"Town of a Thousand," 15
TOWNS, 15–20
TRADE, 62–63
TRANSPORTATION, 62–6[?]
"Traveller's Tree," 10
Tribal distribution, 43
TRIBES, 21–22, 42–44
Tsaratanana Mountains, 6
Tsimihety tribe, 43
Tsiranana Philibert, 29, 32, 33–34, 4[?]
Tsiribihina River, 9
Tuléar, 20
Turtle, 15
University of Tananarive, 35[?]
Unrest, 33–34
Valiha, 55–56
Vanilla, 6, 59
Verreaux's monkey, 13
Vezo clan, 20, 42, 45
"Where There Is Much Salt," 1[?]
Wildlife, 10–15
Witch-doctors, 53–54
Women, 3, 39, 40, 41, 42, 43, 45, 4[?]
WORKING CONDITION[?] AND WELFARE, 3[?]
Zafimaniry clan, 42
Zebu, 42–43, 54, 59–60
Zoma, 16